BLAZERS™

# Disgusting Jobs

BY CONNIE COLWELL MILLER

Capstone
press®

Mankato, Minnesota

Blazers is published by Capstone Press,
151 Good Counsel Drive, P.O. Box 669, Mankato, Minnesota 56002.
www.capstonepress.com

*Library of Congress Cataloging-in-Publication Data*
Miller, Connie Colwell, 1976–
    Disgusting jobs / by Connie Colwell Miller.
    p. cm.—(Blazers. That's disgusting!)
    Includes bibliographical references and index.
    ISBN-13: 978-0-7368-6800-6 (hardcover)
    ISBN-10: 0-7368-6800-3 (hardcover)
    ISBN-13: 978-0-7368-7878-4 (softcover pbk.)
    ISBN-10: 0-7368-7878-5 (softcover pbk.)
    1. Occupations—Miscellanea—Juvenile literature. I. Title.
HF5381.2.M54 2007
331.702—dc22                                                    2006026502

Summary: Describes 10 disgusting jobs and what makes them gross.

**Editorial Credits**
Mandy Robbins, editor; Thomas Emery, designer; Bob Lentz, illustrator;
    Jo Miller, photo researcher/photo editor


**Photo Credits**
Corbis/Franco Vogt, 13; Jeffrey L. Rotman, cover, 9; Raymond Gehman, 22–23;
    Star Ledger/Patti Sapone, 18–19; Ted Soqui, 24–25
Getty Images Inc./AFP/Mahmud Hams, 28–29; Liaison/Stephen Ferry, 14–15
Grant Heilman Photography/Larry Lefever, 20–21
PhotoEdit Inc./Clayton Sharrard, 6–7, 10–11, 26–27; Skjold Photographs, 16–17
Phototake/CMP Images/Pulse Picture Library, 4–5

1 2 3 4 5 6 12 11 10 09 08 07

# Table of Contents

# That's Disgusting!

Lab workers take pee samples from patients and run tests on them.

Would you dress a dead person or walk through mounds of trash? Believe it or not, it is some people's jobs to do these things.

GROSS-O-METER

Use this meter to gauge how disgusting these jobs really are.

THAT'S DISGUSTING

# Diaper Duty

Day care workers get to play with kids all day. But they also have to change dirty diapers and clean up puke.

## GROSS-O-METER

SORT OF DISGUSTING

# BLAZER FACT

Newborn babies poop about 10 times a day. And they don't even eat solid food!

# Bug Off!

Most people keep away from rats, bats, and bugs. But exterminators seek them out. They catch or kill pests with traps and poison.

## GROSS-O-METER

SORT OF DISGUSTING

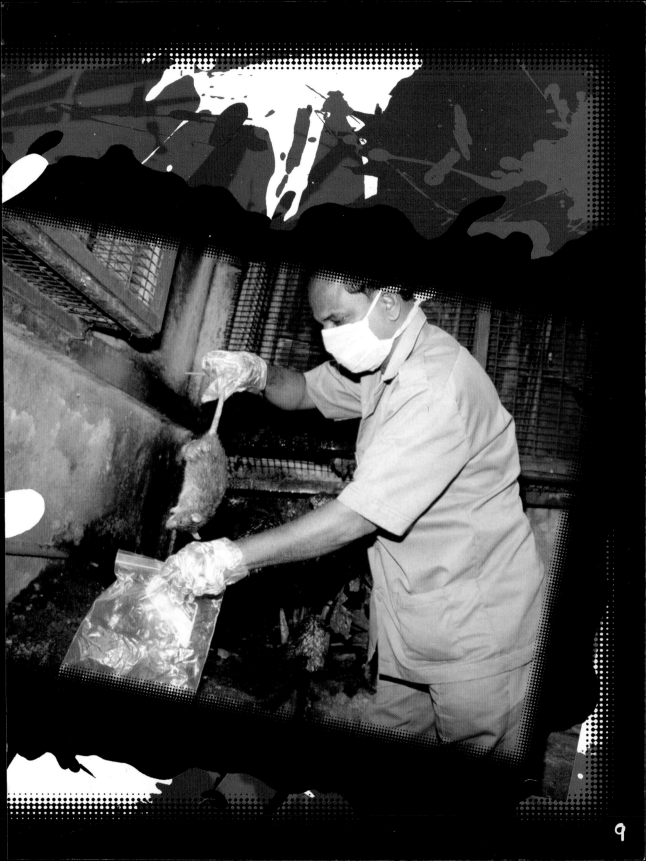

9

# Dog Days

Workers at animal shelters clean up after animals. They scoop out litter boxes and hose down dog kennels.

GROSS-O-METER

SORT OF DISGUSTING

# Toe Jam

Feet can be sweaty, smelly, and scaly. Pedicurists rub, scrub, and paint toenails on feet of all shapes and sizes.

GROSS-O-METER

SORT OF DISGUSTING

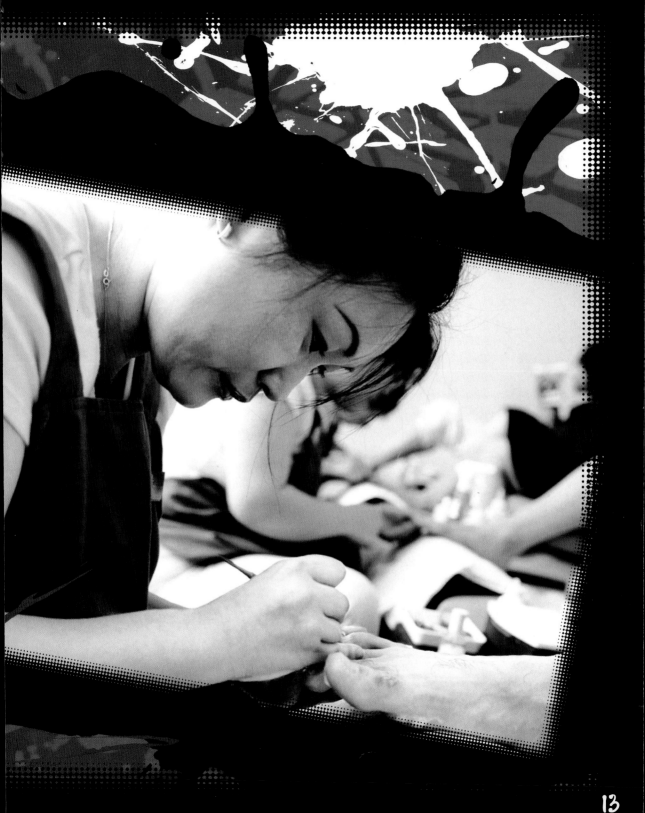

# Rotten Work

Landfill monitors test the soil and water near garbage dumps. Rats scurry around them as the smell of rotting trash fills the air.

GROSS-O-METER

PRETTY DISGUSTING

# Potty Time!

Some people have the unlucky job of cleaning outdoor toilets. They pick up dirty toilet paper and scrub inside the unit.

**GROSS-O-METER**

PRETTY DISGUSTING

Huge hoses suck human waste out of toilets.

# Body Work

Cosmetic surgeons suck out fat and cut off extra skin. They do these and many other disgusting things to make people feel beautiful.

PRETTY DISGUSTING

GROSS-O-METER

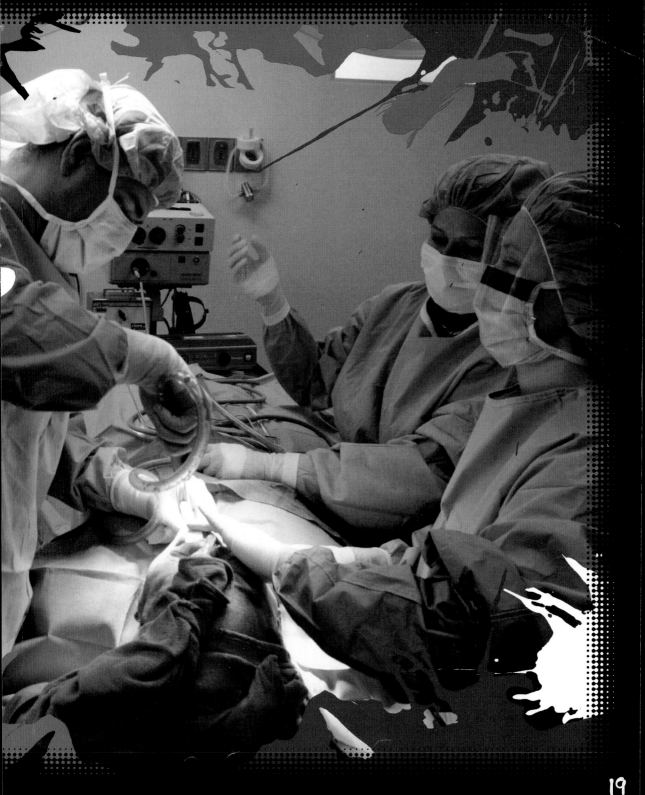

# Hog Wild

Hog farmers work in a stinky cloud of fumes. Hog poop turns into a sloppy soup that smells awful.

## GROSS-O-METER

REALLY DISGUSTING

Fumes from hog farms can make people sick!

# Road Kill

Highway workers pick up dead animals on the road. Blood and guts are often splattered across the pavement.

GROSS-O-METER

REALLY DISGUSTING

# It's a Crime

When a deadly crime occurs, a bloody mess may be left behind. Crime scene cleaners need strong cleaning supplies and strong stomachs.

GROSS-O-METER

REALLY DISGUSTING

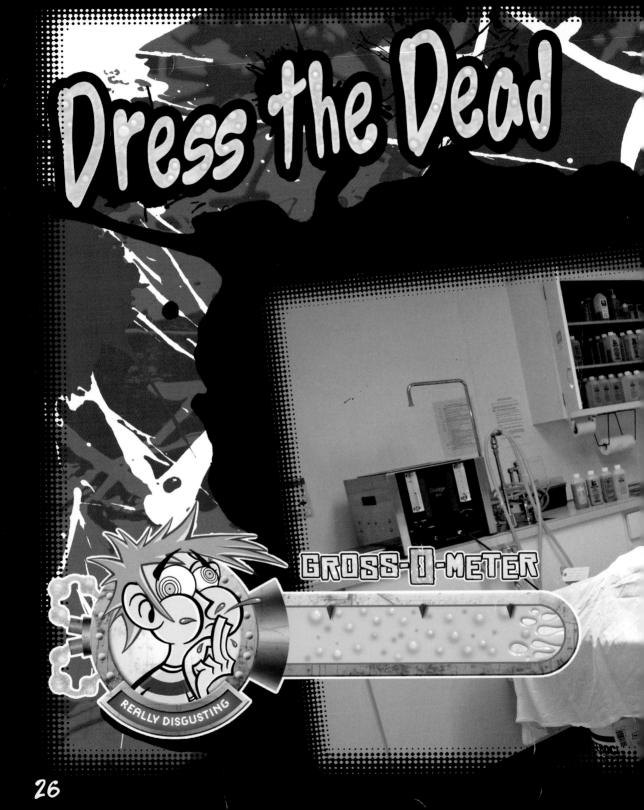

# Dress the Dead

**GROSS-O-METER**

REALLY DISGUSTING

Morticians prepare dead bodies for viewing at funerals. They apply makeup, comb hair, and dress the dead people.

Morticians put chemicals inside dead bodies to preserve them.

27

# Dirty Work

Workers at chicken farms reach under chickens to collect eggs.

The world is a messy place. Someone has to do the dirty work. People who do disgusting jobs help make our lives better.

We made it through, and I have one thing to say. **That's disgusting!**

# Glossary

**exterminator** (ek-STUR-muh-nay-tur)—a person who rids places of unwanted pests for a living

**fume** (FYOOM)—unpleasant or harmful gas, smoke, or vapor given off by something burning or by chemicals

**monitor** (MON-uh-tur)—a person who keeps track of a place or a situation

**mortician** (mor-TISH-uhn)—a person who prepares dead bodies for funerals

**preserve** (pri-ZURV)—to protect something so that it does not spoil or rot

# Read More

**Masoff, Joy.** *Oh, Yuck! The Encyclopedia of Everything Nasty.* New York: Workman, 2000.

**O'Shei, Tim.** *The World's Most Dangerous Jobs.* The World's Top Tens. Mankato, Minn.: Capstone Press, 2007.

**Szpirglas, Jeff.** *Gross Universe: Your Guide to All Disgusting Things Under the Sun.* Toronto: Maple Tree Press, 2004.

# Internet Sites

FactHound offers a safe, fun way to find Internet sites related to this book. All of the sites on FactHound have been researched by our staff.

Here's how:

1. Visit *www.facthound.com*

2. Choose your grade level.

3. Type in this book ID **0736868003** for age-appropriate sites. You may also browse subjects by clicking on letters, or by clicking on pictures and words.

4. Click on the **Fetch It** button.

**FactHound will fetch the best sites for you!**

# Index